Seasonal Crafts

Winter

Gillian Chapman

RSVP
RAINTREE
STECK-VAUGHN
PUBLISHERS
The Steck-Vaughn Company

Austin, Texas

8171019

Seasonal Crafts

Spring • Summer • Autumn • Winter

Published by Raintree Steck-Vaughn Publishers, an imprint of Steck-Vaughn Company

Printed in Italy. Bound in the United States.
1 2 3 4 5 6 7 8 9 0 02 01 00 99 98

Library of Congress Cataloging-in-Publication Data
Chapman, Gillian.
Winter / Gillian Chapman.
    p.   cm.—(Seasonal crafts)
Includes bibliographical references and index.
Summary: Provides directions for creating crafts, including mobiles, cards, and slippers, for the winter season and comments on its events and festivals.
ISBN 0-8172-4871-4
1. Holiday decorations—Juvenile literature.
2. Handicraft—Juvenile literature.
3. Winter—Juvenile literature.
[1. Holiday decorations. 2. Handicraft. 3. Winter.]
I. Title.
TT900.H6C49   1998
745.594'1—dc21   97-4059

Picture acknowledgments:
B & C Alexander 22; Circa 20 (John Smith); E.T. Archive 10, 24; the Hutchison Library 16; Photri 6, 8; Robert Harding (Ching Mai) 28; Tony Stone Worldwide 4 (Stephen Studd), 18 (Robert Shafter), 26 (David Young Wolff); Zefa 12. All commissioned photography, including the cover pictures, by Chris Fairclough. Props made by Gillian Chapman.

Contents

Words that are shown in **bold** are explained in the glossary on page 31.

Winter Time

△ *People enjoy playing in the snow. In this park they are sledding down the snowy slopes.*

In many countries winter can be a very cold time of year. People dress in layers of heavy clothes to keep warm. Some animals and plants spend the season resting. This is their way of escaping from the cold snow and frost when the ground is frozen and there is little food to eat.

Candles and fireplaces are an important part of winter. In the past, lighting fires and candles were the only ways to have light and warmth. In winter celebrations, the flames of fire are **symbolic**. Fire shows the power that light has over darkness and evil spirits.

Winter Projects

Winter Festivities

Christmas and New Year festivals are times of great celebration all over the world. People decorate their homes, have parties, and exchange presents and cards.

Recycling Christmas

After Christmas is over, all the wrapping papers, greeting cards, and empty present boxes are usually thrown away. But they can all be recycled and used again. Some of the projects in this book will show you how.

Old cards and gift wrap can all be used to make gift boxes, cards, and decorations for next Christmas. Start to make a collection now.

Paints and Glues

Poster and powder paints are ideal for most projects. Having different-sized paintbrushes is helpful, and felt-tipped pens can be used for fine detail.

Keep old brushes for gluing. Glue will hold thick cardboard together. Mix it with water to make papier-mâché. Use a glue stick for paper and poster board.

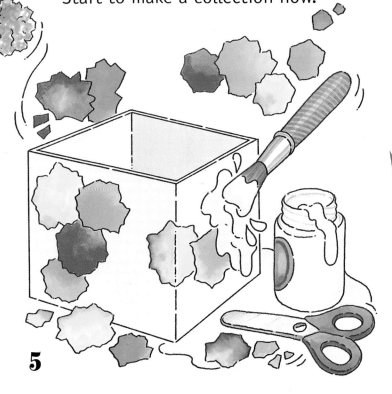

Thanksgiving

Thanksgiving is held on the fourth Thursday in November. It is the day when families enjoy roast turkey and pumpkin pie and remember their **ancestors** who sailed to America from Europe in December 1620.

When the Pilgrims arrived, it was too cold to plant seeds. Many settlers died, but others were helped through the harsh winter by the **Native Americans**. In the spring the Pilgrims planted crops. They held the first Thanksgiving Feast in 1621 to celebrate a good harvest and to thank the Native Americans.

A family sits around the table together to enjoy a traditional Thanksgiving meal. ▽

Making a Pop-up Turkey Card

1 Fold one sheet of paper in half. Cut a strip of paper 1 in. wide and half the length of the sheet. ▽

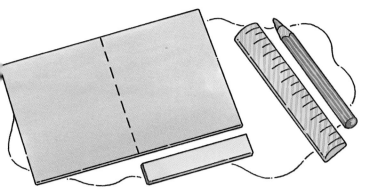

You will need:
* Construction paper
* Scissors
* Pencil and ruler
* Glue stick
* Construction paper scraps

2 Fold the strip of paper in half. Fold back each end by $1/2$ in. ▽

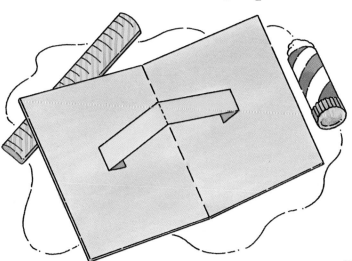

4 Cut out a circle of paper, fold it in half, and glue it to the strip. Make sure the folds line up. ▽

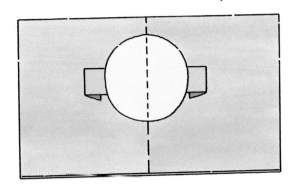

5 Decorate the card by gluing on shapes cut from colored paper. ▽

3 Lay the strip across the center of the paper, lining up the center folds. Glue the strip to the paper. △

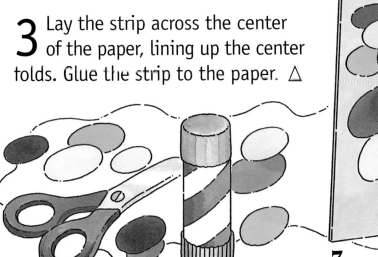

Advent

Advent is the time leading up to Christmas. The name means "the coming." It is when Christians prepare to celebrate the birth of Jesus Christ.

In Europe and the United States Advent is celebrated by decorating homes and churches with candles and wreaths. The wreath has four candles, and one is lit for each Sunday in Advent. Advent calendars are a popular way to count the days until Christmas begins.

A child lights the candles on the Advent wreath in her church. ▽

Making an Advent Cascade

You will need:

* 24 small boxes
* 24 wrapped candies
* Christmas gift wrap, ribbon, and tinsel
* Scissors
* Tape
* Labels and pen
* Wire coat hanger

1 Put a piece of candy into each of the small boxes. Wrap them in the gift wrap. ▽

2 Tie the boxes with the ribbon and label them, marking each with a number 1 to 24. Tie a piece of ribbon to each box, and attach it to the coat hanger. ▽

3 Tie all the boxes to the coat hanger, hanging them at different lengths. ▷

4 Cover the wire coat hanger with extra ribbon or tinsel. Decorate it with any spare decorations. Hang the Advent Cascade and open a box on each day of Advent. ▽

St. Nicholas's Day

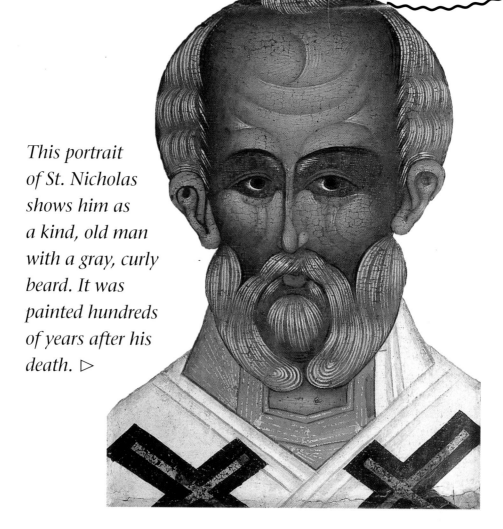

This portrait of St. Nicholas shows him as a kind, old man with a gray, curly beard. It was painted hundreds of years after his death. ▷

This is the feast day of St. Nicholas, who died on December 6 in A.D. 326. He was a Turkish **bishop**, who is remembered for being kind and generous to children.

Stories tell us that St. Nicholas used to leave small presents in children's shoes. In many northern European countries, people give presents on this day. In Amsterdam, a city in the Netherlands, there is a parade and "St. Nicholas" rides into the city on a white horse, led by his servant, Black Peter.

Making St. Nicholas's Slippers

1 To make a slipper pattern, draw an oval shape onto a piece of scrap cardboard and cut it out. ▽

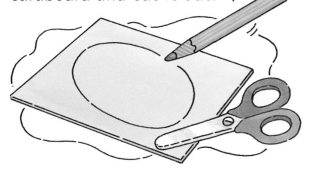

2 Use the pattern to make the felt shapes. Place the pattern on the felt. Trace around it and cut out the felt oval shapes. Repeat until you have three felt ovals. ▽

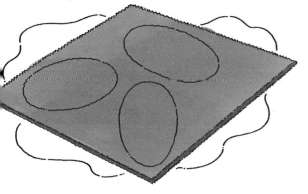

4 Glue felt shapes onto the toe with rubber cement. ▽

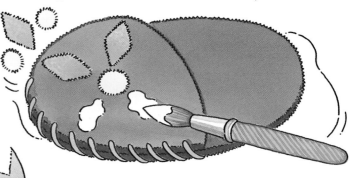

5 Make a small hole in the slipper and thread the ribbon through. Make a second slipper the same way. Fill the slippers with candy and hang them on the tree. ▽

3 Cut one of the felt ovals in half and pin it on top of another. Then neatly sew them together. ▽

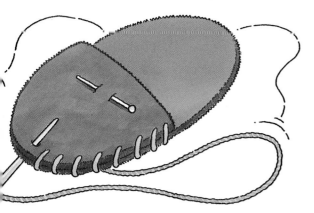

Hanukkah

△ *During Hanukkah the smallest candle on the **menorah** is used to light one candle each night until all eight are alight.*

Hanukkah is the Jewish Festival of Lights, which lasts for eight days in December. Over 2,000 years ago, a small Jewish army defeated the **Syrian** army in battle. The Jews returned to their temple to find only one lamp of holy oil left. But by a **miracle** of God, the flame burned for eight days until more oil could be found.

During Hanukkah Jewish people remember this miracle by lighting a candle on a **menorah**. There is one candle for each day of the festival. Families also celebrate by exchanging cards and gifts.

Making a Hanukkah Card

The six-pointed Star of David is an important Jewish symbol. This card uses the star as part of the design.

1 To make a six-pointed star, first draw a circle on the paper with a compass. ▽

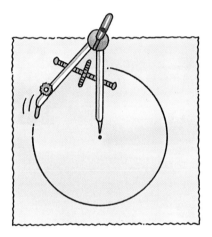
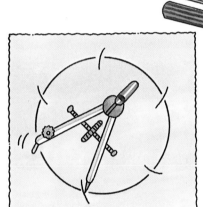
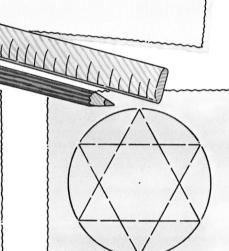

2 Use the compass to divide the circle **circumference** into six equal parts. △

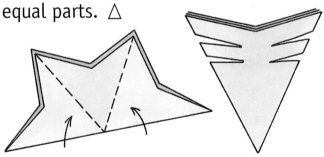

3 Connect the points to form a star. Then cut it out. △

4 Fold the star in half and then in thirds. Carefully cut small slits in each side. Open the star and fold back the slits. △

5 Fold a rectangle of paper in half and glue the star to the front. ▷

Christmas Decorations

In the weeks before Christmas, people prepare for the holiday by decorating their homes. Here are some ideas for making decorations from scraps of Christmas ribbons, gift wrap, and candy wrappers.

Making Festive Chains

1 Use scraps of different-colored Christmas ribbons and cut them into 6-in. pieces. ▷

2 Curl the first piece of ribbon and either staple or glue it together. Attach more pieces to make a chain. ▷

Making Christmas Lanterns

1 Flatten a scrap of gift wrap, with the decorated side facing down. Glue a piece of paper to it. When the glue dries, cut off the extra gift wrap. ▷

2 Fold the gift wrap in half and make a series of cuts along the length. Then glue the sides together and staple a handle to the top. ▷

You will need:
* Scraps of Christmas gift wrap and ribbons
* Construction paper
* Scissors
* Stapler
* Glue stick

14

Making Dancing Animals

1 Draw a simple animal shape on dark cardboard with a light-colored pencil. Then cut it out. △

2 Cut shapes out of the animal with scissors or a hole punch. △

3 Turn the animal over and carefully stick pieces of colored candy wrappers over the holes, using small drops of glue. △

4 Cut out extra details, like antlers, and glue them in place. Attach the ribbon and hang the dancing animal in the window or on the Christmas tree. ▽

Mexican Christmas

In Mexico many kinds of colorful Christmas decorations are made from clay and are brightly painted. These are sold in markets during the weeks before Christmas. Colorful piñatas are also made as part of the preparations for Christmas. These are hollow paper animals, filled with candy or coins, which are hung up as centerpieces at parties.

At the end of the Christmas celebrations, children are blindfolded and have great fun by trying to break open the piñatas with a stick. When the piñata breaks, it showers candy and coins all over the party guests.

This colorful Mexican market stall is full of little painted figures that people can buy for their Nativity scenes. ▽

Making a Christmas Piñata

1 Tear old newspapers into strips and glue them over the blown-up balloon. ▽

You will need:
* Newspapers
* Diluted glue
* Blown-up balloon
* Powder paint and brush
* Christmas decorations: tinsel, streamers, and ribbons
* Chocolate coins
* Stick and blindfold

2 Cover the balloon completely with about three layers of glued newspapers, and let it dry. △

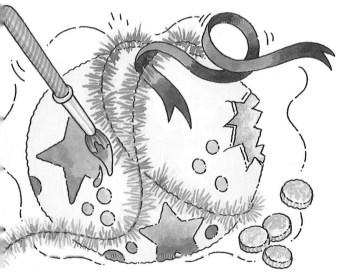

3 Pop the balloon with a pin. Then decorate your piñata. Paint patterns with the powder paint and glue on the tinsel and ribbons. △

4 Put the chocolate coins inside and fill the hole with crumpled paper. Hang the piñata at your party and have fun trying to break it open! ▽

Christmas Trees

△ *A large house is beautifully decorated for Christmas with lights, garlands, and wreaths.*

Christmas is one of the most important holidays of the Christian year. Streets and houses are decorated with colored lights and Christmas trees. It is a time of great joy and celebration, when people remember their family and friends with cards, gifts, and parties.

Although Kwanzaa is not a Christmas holiday, it begins on December 26. Kwanzaa is really a harvest festival. It is also a time when African Americans celebrate their history. Kwanzaa was first celebrated in 1966.

Making a Christmas Table Tree

1 Make a pattern by drawing a tree shape onto scrap cardboard. Cut out the pattern and use it to make three trees from the green cardboard. ▽

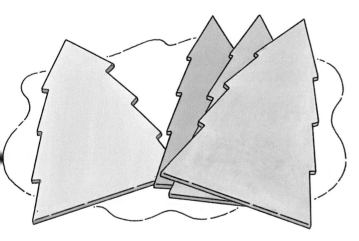

2 Fold the trees in half and give the center fold a good crease. Put them on top of one another and hold in place with paper clips. ▽

4 Then open out the sections and attach the chocolates to the cardboard with small pieces of double-sided tape. ▽

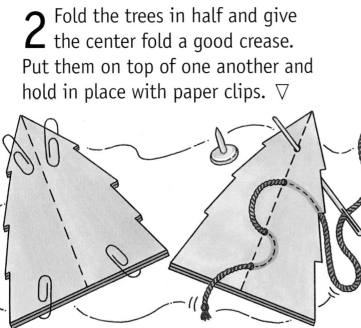

3 Make four holes along the center crease with the drawing pin. Make sure the pin goes through all the trees. Sew the thread through these holes to hold the trees together. △

Twelfth Night

△ *The story of the three kings, Caspar, Melchior, and Balthasar, visiting baby Jesus, is told by these children in their Nativity Play.*

The twelfth night after Christmas is the Christian feast of Epiphany. The three kings visited Jesus in the stable at Bethlehem on that night and gave Him gifts of gold, **frankincense**, and **myrrh**.

Twelfth Night is the last day of the Christmas holiday. Families take down all the Christmas decorations, clean up their homes, and look forward to the new year.

Making Christmas Boxes and Cards

Here are some ideas for using all the scraps of Christmas paper that are usually thrown away. Make these colorful Christmas boxes and cards for next year!

1 Collect all the scraps of wrapping paper, labels, and old cards that are no longer wanted and cut out all the Christmas pictures. △

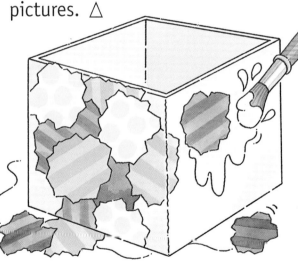

2 Choose a box to cover, and glue the pictures to the box. Start on one side, overlapping the pictures so the cardboard does not show. △

3 Completely cover the box and lid with pictures and protect the decorated box with a varnish made from glue mixed with water. ▽

4 Make labels and cards by using the cut-out pictures and gluing them to folded rectangles of construction paper. ▽

Winter Stories

Winter in the **Arctic** is very long and harsh. Days are short because it gets dark in the early afternoon. For the people who live in these regions, the long, dark winter nights are a time for telling stories.

Many years ago the **Inuit** women used to tell stories and legends with little finger puppets that help bring the stories to life. Their legends were often about the creatures and spirits of their lands. They told stories about the moon and stars and about the animals of the Arctic: the seal, walrus, whale, and **caribou**.

A Saami (Lapp) family living in a traditional tent in northern Norway. Today most families live in modern houses with central heating. ▽

Making Finger Puppets

You will need:
* Construction paper
* Compass
* Pencil and ruler
* Scissors
* Glue stick
* Tape
* Large ring pulls

1 Draw circles that measure 4 in. across onto construction paper and cut them out. △

2 Cut out pieces of construction paper and glue them to the circles. Make them into faces or figures. △

3 Tape two ring pulls to each face to put your fingers through. △

Try making different kinds of animal faces and figures. Then tell a story about them and bring them to life with your fingers.

New Year's Day

△ *A bronze Roman coin shows the two faces of the god, Janus, looking backward to the past and forward to the future.*

Many people celebrate New Year's Day on January 1. Others use a different calendar. Some people use the **lunar** calendar, which is based on **phases** of the moon. The dates of these holidays change from year to year.

Julius Caesar started the **Gregorian** calendar. January is named after the Roman god Janus. He had two faces. One looked backward on the old year, the other looked forward to the new one. January 1 was a public holiday in ancient Rome, and still is today. At midnight on New Year's Eve, people celebrate with parties and fireworks to welcome the New Year.

Making a Star Mobile

1 Using the method shown on page 13, draw a large star onto the cardboard and cut it out. ▽

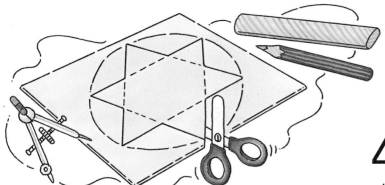

You will need:
* Colored cardboard scraps
* Compass
* Pencil and scissors
* Glue stick
* Hole punch
* Thin colored string

2 Draw smaller circles and star shapes on the colored cardboard, using the compass. Then cut them all out. ▽

4 Use the hole punch to make holes in the large star and the other shapes. Then tie the shapes to the star with different lengths of string. Try threading several stars to one piece of string. Then hang up your star mobile. ▽

3 To make the sun and planets decorate some of the circles with scraps of cardboard. ▽

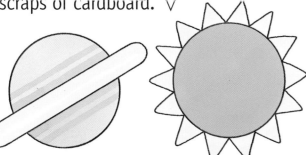

Yuan Tan

△ *Chinese New Year is celebrated all over the world, with colorful, embroidered costumes and parades, like this one in Los Angeles.*

Chinese New Year is the most important Chinese festival, and it lasts for fifteen days. All Chinese birthdays are held during this time, so there is special food, family parties, street parades, and fireworks. Children are given presents of "lucky money" in red and gold envelopes.

Each year is named after twelve animals—the rat, ox, tiger, hare, dragon, snake, horse, ram, monkey, rooster, dog, and pig. Each of these has a characteristic—the tiger is brave and the dog is loyal. People who are born in the year of a particular animal are said to be like it.

Making a Chinese Birthday Card

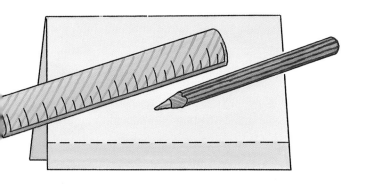

You will need:
* Construction paper
* Pencil and scissors
* Ruler
* Glue stick
* Construction paper scraps

1 Fold a sheet of paper in half. Draw a dotted line along each side of the card, $1/2$ in. from the edge. △

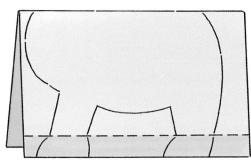

2 Draw a simple animal shape on the folded paper. Choose one of the Chinese birthday animals, like the tiger. Make sure the paws are drawn below the dotted line. △

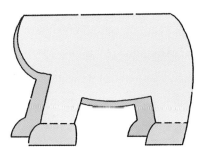

3 Cut out the animal, making sure to cut through both sides of the card. Do not cut along the top fold. △

4 Decorate the animal with scraps of paper. Glue on the ears and a tail. △

5 Fold the paws out to make the animal card stand up. Open the card to write a message inside. ▽

27

Teng Chien

Teng Chien is the Chinese Lantern Festival. It takes place on the fifteenth, and final, day of the Chinese New Year. Animal-shaped lanterns are carried through the streets. These lights symbolize the coming of spring.

The Dance of the Dragon is the most important part of the festival, when huge dragons, symbols of good luck, dance through the streets. The dragon costumes are made from bamboo and colored silk. They can be up to one hundred feet long and need many dancers inside to carry them.

A huge Chinese dragon dances through the streets of Singapore with lots of fireworks. ▽

Making a Dancing Dragon Mask

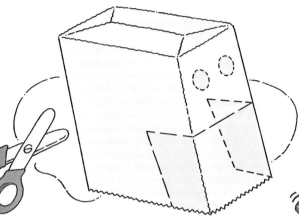

1 Make sure the bag is big enough to go over your head. Cut out a section from the front to make the dragon's snout and cut out holes for the nostrils. △

3 Using the sharp pencil point, carefully make a hole in each Ping-Pong ball and also on each side of the bag. Thread one end of the tag through the hole in the ball and the other through the bag to make the dragon's eyes. △

2 Paint the bag to cover up any printing. When the paint has dried, decorate the bag with shapes cut from the construction paper. Cut out ears, teeth, and scales and glue them to the mask with the glue stick. △

4 Roll strips of construction paper around the pencil to make the dragon's mane. Attach the strips to the head with tape. Now the dragon is ready to dance! △

29

Winter Calendar

This calendar refers only to events and festivals mentioned in this book.

Thanksgiving Day
Fourth Thursday in November
First Day of Advent
December 1
St. Nicholas's Day
December 6
Hanukkah (The Jewish Festival of Lights)
Celebrated for 8 days in December
Christmas Day
December 25
New Year's Day
January 1
Twelfth Night
January 6
Yuan Tan (The Chinese New Year)
Celebrated for 15 days in January
Teng Chien (The Chinese Lantern Festival)
Last Day of Yuan Tan

(Many religions and cultures use the lunar calendar, which means that their festivals are not held on the same day every year.)

Glossary

ancestors Relatives that lived many years ago.

Arctic The polar region, near the North Pole.

bishop A high priest in the Christian Church.

caribou A herd of reindeer.

circumference The measurement around a circle or sphere.

frankincense A special type of incense.

Gregorian The calendar that usually has 365 days in a year.

Inuit People who live in the Arctic regions.

lunar Controlled by the moon.

menorah A Jewish candlestick with eight branches.

miracle When something unbelievable and wonderful happens.

myrrh A sweet-smelling gum used to make incense.

Native American People who lived in America before settlers arrived.

phases The changes in the movement of the moon.

symbolic Something that has a special meaning.

Syrian People who come from Syria, a country in the Middle East.

Further Reading

Blackwood, Alan. *New Year.* Holidays and Festivals. Vero Beach, FL: Rourke Publishing Group, 1987.

Chin, Steven A. *Dragon Parade: A Chinese New Year Story.* Stories of America. Austin, TX: Raintree Steck-Vaughn, 1992.

Corwin, Judith H. *Thanksgiving Fun.* Holiday Library. Parsippany, NJ: Silver Burdett Press, 1984.

Devonshire, Hilary, et. al. *Christmas Crafts.* Fresh Start. Danbury, CT: Franklin Watts, 1990.

Kalman, Bobbie. *We Celebrate Hanukkah.* Holidays and Festivals. New York: Crabtree Publishing Co., 1986.

Lankford, Mary D. *Christmas Around the World.* New York: Morrow Junior Books, 1995.

Index